Alibis and Lies

Rózália Sófalvi

iUniverse, Inc.
Bloomington

Alibis and Lies

Visit the author on Facebook.
Write to her at:
rozalia_sofalvi@hotmail.com

Photograph of the author by J. C. Elvy
Cover photograph by Rózália Sófalvi

iUniverse books may be ordered through booksellers or by contacting:

iUniverse
1663 Liberty Drive
Bloomington, IN 47403
www.iuniverse.com
1-800-Authors (1-800-288-4677)

ISBN: 978-1-4502-8477-6 (sc)
ISBN: 978-1-4502-8478-3 (dj)
ISBN: 978-1-4502-8479-0 (ebk)

Printed in the United States of America

iUniverse rev. date: 2/9/2011

For Jonathan, Sarah, and Aiden
who remind me every day
of what is important and real.

RÓZÁLIA SÓFALVI writes simple poems about the most complex thing in life: our universal search for love. Her words resonate on our tongues and in our hearts like melodies we all learned long ago, the soaring tunes and the clashing discords that express our joys and our fears. Sometimes she speaks with the safe perspective of distance from a broken affair, and we nod sagely with her, remembering a lost lover seen only in retrospective; on other pages we are tossed about with her in the tumult of present lives, living the trauma and tears and tenderness through her poet's gift for ragged transparency.

Born into the joyous life of a small Transylvanian village, Rózália was surrounded with loving people, music, conversation and laughter. Wrenched from there at seven and relocated to farm life in southern Ontario, she was immediately isolated by the language barrier, and the strangely serious, foreign new world. Outwardly a sunny girl, she learned, as poets often do, to cry silent tears, to turn her sadness inward, to the fantasy world of hidden thoughts and dreams. Every page in her school notebooks bore evidence of this tear in the fabric of her existence— the physics of stars on one half, dreams and desires on the overleaf.

Beyond school, science long discarded, Rózália keeps a journal of emotions, of fantasies—the hope of finding that special person, a hopefulness which fills all of our minds. For years she wrote her poems only on loose leaves she then threw away, not wanting anyone to know what was in her heart or on her mind. Then a good friend, Carol, inspired her to keep her writings in a real notebook, and so began the collection of *Alibis and Lies*.

As we read the clashing notes of Rózália's fantasies and realities, we are reminded that the journey to love is most often a breathless course through alibis and lies; that perfection, even when we catch a glimpse, is not a forever thing. *Alibis and Lies* is everyone's story. We are not alone in our search. There is always hope. And the search is worth the journey.

Chapter One:
Alibis & Lies

ghosts
fantasies
every moment
filled with uncertainty.

attempts
failures
doubts
secrets...

Alibis.

Where were you
3 a.m. Friday?

You were here.

I remember
holding you.

Rózália Sófalvi

Feeling so good
so warm
so whole
wrapped in your arms
your chest my pillow
your heartbeat my lullaby.

Sleep my love.

I will lie awake enjoying your warmth.

You are here forever.

Tomorrow need not come.

The morning sun rises too soon.
Shatters my crystal dreams.

"Your dreams are just that
… dreams.

They will destroy you."

Morning sun.
Reality.

Go to hell.

Let me lie here
enjoying the warmth
of this man.

Destroy
someone else
today.

Don't laugh
when you see
the crazy things I do.

All the ways
I try to get to you.

I'm just a woman in love.

One of the most pleasant
nights of your life.

That night.

In front of the fireplace...
wine
poetry
romance....

This is me.
My life.

I offered myself
exposed.

Do you like what I am?

If not
you would not like
the person I pretended to be.

Not for any length of time anyway.

Face
flushed.
Heart beating to
the rhythm of your song.

Surely
you know.

Childish though this may seem
or overindulgence in
another fantasy...

I do not care.

Romantic fool
I've been called.

Yes.
I will admit to that.
But I know where reality lies.

I have felt the dagger
thrust into my heart often enough.
Knowing it was there
but turning my back
then awaiting the pain.

It has been so long
since I bared my soul
since I dared tell someone
how I once loved
with the innocence of a child.

Then...

Alibis & Lies

I lay back
(as I often do for Carol
who smiles at me, saying,
"I wish I had a camera so I could
show you how happy you look
when you're so high.")

I listened to your stories
with a starving mind
curious
aroused
awaiting another tale of adventure
(you are a pirate on the high seas,
Sir Lancelot, Robin Hood,
or Houdini...)

Yes.
This must be love.

My pain
my tears disappeared as you talked.
I can't get enough.
I can scarcely breathe.

Surely
you are a fantasy
or a tempting dish
placed before me...

poisoned.

Tempting me.
Teasing me.
You are in complete control.
I am at your mercy
on my knees
head bowed
awaiting the sword
that will crown me
or kill me....

Instead
I feel your feather-light strokes
at the back of my neck.
I hear your soft low voice
as it lures me into a world
high above this world....

Yes.

This must be love.

Mesmerized.
Your eyes
draw me
deeper and deeper
into an unreal world.

Farther and farther
from the world I know.
Your fingers
draw me
toward a kiss
I know could kill.

I cannot fight.

I hear a voice
somewhere
deep inside.

But voices
have no place
in this passion.

Yes.

If, indeed, this is a fantasy....

You sweep me into your arms.
Carry me to my bed.
Where
you
gently
lay me.

Romantic fool?

Yes.

But I know
where
reality
lies.

I don't like pulling back
when a door opens.

Feeling guilt
for enjoying
an embrace
or a kiss.

But
for you
I do.

You see me
strong
and alone
able to conquer the world
on my own.

Look a little deeper, darling.

My conquests mean
nothing
without
you.

I need to talk to you.

I feel lost.
Alone.

No one else understands
you
me
music.

Music
magic that makes me
forget pain
for a second
then brings it
crashing back.

Heaven.
Hell.
Nowhere
between.

Music.

Alibis & Lies

You think
I'm brave and strong
because
I let you go?

Don't you know
how hard it is
to watch you turn
and walk away?

There hasn't been
enough time.

We haven't said
all we meant to say.

I love you.

Please stay.

There will never be
enough time.
To say everything.
To do everything.

Life is short.

Rózália Sófalvi

Clinging to you
desperately.

Please don't leave me now.
Please don't ever leave me.

"You know I have to go."

Yes.
Damn it!

I am
the understanding woman.
Your friend.

Doesn't it matter
that I need you
with me
tonight?

Perhaps
it would be best
to let you
fade into the
past?

Back to when
you were
a fantasy.

I felt no pain then.

Actions speak louder than words.

Is that how you love?

Free man?

Don't use me

as an

alibi.

Our idea
of a good time
differs.

You get stoned.

I get depressed.

Rózália Sófalvi

Finally tears
allowed to flow freely.

I am no longer
on display.

Must all wounds be visible?

Your pain is self-imposed.

Rózália Sófalvi

Remembering moments
from the past.
Precious moments
when you used to call me friend.

Lying in the car.
Looking up at a starlit
Hamilton sky.

Sharing truths.
You held me in your arms.
Said it was all right.
You understood.

And then
again
you had to leave.

I held on desperately.

Please don't leave me yet.

My tears came.
You comforted me.

I believe you cried too.

You invaded my mind
my whole being.
Then left me open to pain.

You tempt me.
Torment me.
Then cast me aside.

Still I return
for one more glimpse
of the love-light
that once shone
in your eyes.

Rózália Sófalvi

Touching you sets me on fire.
I cannot see.
Cannot think.

I need you.

You leave me shattered.
Defeated.

Standing
half naked
barefoot in the snow.
Tears streaming down my face.

What is left to say
but goodbye?

There must be
a world
beyond
those baby blues.
But
I'm not ready
to look yet.

So difficult to say goodbye.

Savage desire to succeed.
No time to see—
to feel—

Sit down awhile.
Take my hand.

What do you see?

Pretty lights?

You're stoned again.

Rózália Sófalvi

Go away.

You make me angry.

Words fail me
when I need
them
most.

Tough lady
in control of the game.
Play with me.
I love the ecstasy—
the pain.
Touch me.
Make me cry out for you.
Make me want more
than you can give
then
let me down
as lovers
always do.

Your kisses—
the kind I have always craved.
Speaking of love
the wrong place
the wrong time
passion
loneliness.....

Just like old friends.

I spoke of my new love
(afraid to mention his name
...afraid he too might vanish.)

You were pleased
by the smile on my face.

Just like old friends.

Then you pulled me close...
held me tighter than ever before.
You smiled a smile
that seemed
a little forced—

Then you kissed me
with a kiss
that made me forget for a moment
that you were
a married man.

And later
all those
promises
of letters to come
of the time we would spend together....

But darling

I've heard all that
before.

Somewhere
not so far away
yet too far
I picture you
watching shadows of the past
projected in your mind.

Images of
alibis and lies.

Where am I tonight?

Dreaming of you and how it used to be.

Do you lie there believing
in your vows?
(Is she asleep?)
Take care she never reads
your mind.
Don't talk in your dreams
when you remember the woman
who waited for you with open arms.
Whose smiling eyes
used to smile for you.

Forgive me
for my cruelty
and insults.

It seems
I am not as understanding
as you thought.

With or without you

life goes on.

You do not belong in my thoughts.

Dreams have a way
of destroying
what could be
real.

The end to another story.

C'est la vie.

He says
he just
wants to be friends.

Of course, it hurts.

I
should have been
the one
to end it.

Alibis & Lies

Another glass of wine
and I'm feeling strong again.

Let's discuss being alone
in a room filled
with people.

Looking for answers
never to be found.

Reaching out to catch
a falling star.

Funny.

You could have gone so far.

Chapter Two:

More Alibis & Lies

You came off the stage
singing "Wild Eyes".
Slid comfortably
into the chair next to mine
as if you belonged there.

"I'm glad you came back tonight."

I felt pleased.
Very in control.

You had eyes only for me.

Rózália Sófalvi

photographs
fantasies
imagination
fragmented
to form a collage
of life

kaleidoscope images
laughter
tears

Reminiscing...
that kiss from long ago.

Your kiss.

Stepping back.

Examining my past.

My hopes
for the future.

As if seeing you
for the first time.

Afraid.

Opening up.

Seeking.

Perhaps finding.

My soulmate.

Promise

you will
never lie to me.

I know
everything is transient.

Yet...

I believe in romance.
And lifelong love.

Searching desperately
for answers.

I long to forget the past.
Forget the pain.
To start fresh
with you.

Reality—
your phone call.

Trembling.
I explain what is
important.

You listen.

Farewell
is such a hard word
for us to say.

You are new.
Unique.
Refreshing.

Our friendship—

promising?

Long, hot summer afternoons.
Wellesley and Yonge.
Our secret rendezvous.

Your eyes
reflecting
all the good things
about me.

Surely
we met before

in another life.

Rózália Sófalvi

Your gift to me—

your time.

Your
precious
caring
time.

Alibis & Lies

You said
I was
magic.

You said you did not know why.

It's nice
to be
magic.

Rózália Sófalvi

So much said
without
giving away
any secrets.

- 74 -

"Nothing
that happened
before we met
matters."

"I know you
only as you've been
since I've known you.
You are special.
You are—
you."

You showed me
the
peace
in silence
the
joy
in songs.

I feel it happening.

Everything unfolding.

"You're the one
with the imagination…."

You listened to
my childhood stories
my insecurities
my love.

You listened to
my every word

as I listened to yours.

Alibis & Lies

You try to guess
what I will say.

We stop
(in the middle of a sentence)
to sing the same tune.

Rózália Sófalvi

"I've been
thinking of you.
The most important
thing at the moment
was to hear
your voice."

Alibis & Lies

Doesn't matter
how tired I am.
How hopeless it all seems.
You only have to say hello—
suddenly the sun's out.

I take a deep
refreshing breath
relax
sit back awhile.

You make my world
a little brighter
my heart
a little kinder.

All I want to do
is hold you.

Have I told you
I think
you're all right?

Always seems
there's nothing to be said at first.

Then
the barriers drop
words flow freely
smiles
tears
release.

As if you'd given me
my freedom...

Freedom
feels
fantastic.

Rózália Sófalvi

Grasping
for a lifeline.
Been so long

alone.

"No need
to be alone
unless you
choose
to be alone."

"No need to be with
people who bring you down
just for the sake
of being with
someone."

"Only surround yourself
with people
who make you feel good.
People are magic.
Your life is magic."

Love need not
or cannot
be forced.

Either it is
or
it isn't.

Our spirits reaching out...
they will recognize
each other.

Beginning to understand
all we can do
is make the
moment count.

Enjoy the moment.

No one can touch
the precious memories
that come from
those moments.

Alibis & Lies

Past
and future
do not
matter.

Rózália Sófalvi

"There is a time
and a place
for all things
including
honesty
secrets
the past
the future
love
lust
and friendship."

Smooth
mellow blues.
The full moon
peeking out
from behind the clouds.

Wind
whispering
warnings.

A storm is
about to break
the spell of spring.

Rózália Sófalvi

When I was a little girl
I dreamt of being a princess...

(Not because I wanted
special treatment
but because I wanted respect.
More than that...
I wanted to be
left alone
to dream my dream
of being a princess....)

Yes.

My blond-haired
blue-eyed prince
igniting the spark
that would be
...my life?

Beauty indeed
is only skin deep.

Life is not simple!

Soulmates are hard to find.

Alibis & Lies

My favorite line:
"I like spending time alone."
While actually thinking:
"Is there another choice?"

People argue
yes
you choose your own destiny.

Not!

If I chose my own destiny
as freely as people claim,
I could...
I would...
at this moment be
sitting next to you.

Holding your hand.

Anticipating
an evening of conversation
and love.

Rózália Sófalvi

No.

Life is not simple.

My
insatiable hunger
for understanding
makes me
less tolerant.

Defeating my purpose.

Rózália Sófalvi

Classy.
Quick.
Bright.
Addictive.

You.

Alibis & Lies

Seated
side by side.

Darkness
all around.

Images
flash across the screen.
(My elbow
brushes
your arm.)

Sounds
loud
loud sounds.
Innocence.
Child.
Misunderstood.
Manchild.
(My hand
brushes
your hand.)

Waiting.

Drawing back.
Uh oh...
we are
supposed to be
friends.

Only friends.

Images
flash across the screen
(hands
fingers
gently touching
lingering
teasing).

"Quadrophenia."
(Eyes closed.
Lips parted.
Anxiously waiting.
Anxiously.
Waiting.)
"Quadrophenia."

Alibis & Lies

Longing.
Searching.
Where do I belong?

Love.
Lost.
Escape.
Life.

Easier to escape life.

Over the wall
falling
falling
falling down.

Silence.
Vacuum.
Chaos.
Death.

End of fear.
End of longing.
End of life.

Friends.
Only friends.

Funny.
Holding on to something
that exists
only in our minds.
Holding on.
Pretending
things are not the way they seem.

They are.

Hard to walk away
after believing for so long.

Was I wrong to believe?

You do not reject me.

Yet I remain
alone.

Crying.
Fists clenched.
Trying
to understand.

Love
is not
to be gained
so easily.

A telephone romance.

Hey baby
wanna take a chance
on a telephone romance?

Listen while
I tease you.
I know
I can please you
in a
telephone romance.

Rózália Sófalvi

It's all right to be a romantic
as long as you are aware
of the consequences
of being a romantic.

Reach out.
But be prepared
to be burned.

Love is described
as a burning, passionate
need.
(Or is that lust?)
Anyway, when you
seek love
you expose yourself
to dangers—
passions
out of control.

Crazy love.
Temporary insanity.

I believe love
is blind.

Depending
on a lover's smile

to make my world complete?

How long does a smile last?

That's like wishing
every day
was filled with sunshine.

We expect
all our needs
to be filled by one person.
Could we fill all the needs
of someone else?
Could we afford to
give that much
of ourselves?

No one else
can fill
our lonely hours.

The past...
experiences
that leave us happy
sad
bitter
afraid
depressed.

Reaching out.

All
we can do is
continue
along the path
we have chosen.

Sooner
or later
someone will join us.

Feverishly writing.

All is relative.

What we are
where we are
constantly changing.

Circumstance
rearranging our lives.

Our lives
seemingly endless
in a second
could be past.

You are on my mind.
Constantly.
I told you a pillow
is not enough to hold
yet
I hold a man—
warm
eager
hard.
And think of you.

I would rather
lie next to you
fully clothed
inhaling you
your arm
around my shoulder...
your fingers touching mine...
than kiss a man
whose passion
burns for a moment
then is cold as ice.

Alibis & Lies

Work.
Boredom.
Moment by moment
I review my financial situation.

I remember you saying
"Hang in there, you'll get used to it."

My bruises….

"I will kiss them better."

My body aches.
Black and blue.
My mind is worn.
My heart aching.

Where are you now?

Your whispered promise
of a possible seduction.

I wish....

Hold on.
Breathe deep.
Everything
does not
need to be today.

Rózália Sófalvi

I have
a dream.

Someday

you will be mine.

Be persistent.

Be patient.

Reassurance—

is that what you need?

Speak to me.

Friends?

Reassure me.

Let's recreate our phone calls....

You said,
"Don't think about it."

How can I not
when you speak of
caressing me
kissing me...
my neck
breasts
stomach
thighs.
Pulling me close.
Loving me all night long.

"Your wish is my command."

Let's go dancing.

"You want to go out with me?"

Yes.
Very much.

"I want to seduce you in your darkroom."

Seduce me on the dance floor.

I never see you.

Alibis & Lies

You lead me on
when you've got nowhere
to take me.

You lead me on
then say I was
mistaken
about love.

Rózália Sófalvi

Phone calls
in the middle of
the night.

Dirty little love lies
to turn me on.

Why awaken
dangerous desires
that can never
be fulfilled?

"I'll make sure it feels good."

If only….

Hell with reason and time.
Come to me
now.

Hold me
the way you told me you would.

Set me free from my fantasies.

Alibis & Lies

Who are we trying to kid?
Playing with emotions.
Leading each other on.
The result can only be pain.

You said calling you
creates problems
for you.

Well...
not calling you
creates problems for me.

I have begun to look
to you
for support.
Or just to share moments.

But good moments
make me want hours.
Smiling makes me want to laugh.

There is
never enough time.

Rózália Sófalvi

How can something
that feels
so good
feel so bad?

So happy to hear from you.
My heart is racing
yet...
I sound angry
bitter
cold.

What's this, my once-a-month
phone call?

"Quarterly, isn't it?"

Stop trying to be funny,
I'm hurting.
Why did you call?

"Just a friendly hello—
to see how you are."

Alibis & Lies

I'm fine.

"Then relax."

I can't.
I'm trying not to be
so intense—
but I'm trembling.
I can't take your phone calls
lightly
anymore.

"Don't you want me to call?"
No.
Yes.
No.
I'd rather see you.

Your phone calls confuse me.
I don't understand you.

"Don't try to understand.
Just answer me.
Don't you like it when I call?"

Yes.
But I'm confused.

Either
you are being deliberately
cruel
or
I misunderstand
your intentions.

Rózália Sófalvi

You have entered my soul.
There is no room for
anyone else
anymore.

I want only you.

You keep your foot in the doorway.
Without entering
or backing out.

Alibis & Lies

I look in the mirror
at eyes
you once said
held a lust for life.

Now.
You are gone.
You have taken my smile—
and the sparkle of my eyes.

Walls get higher
as the days go by.
Hiding from the enemy
but it's inside.

Not letting anyone close anymore.

Looking for a better way
to make it through the days
and the nights
without you
or your phone calls....

But....

No answers can be found
in the crystal ball
that lies at the bottom of
an empty glass.

Rózália Sófalvi

You promised
you would always be my friend.

Can no one be trusted anymore?

To what extent
will desperation take me?

Rózália Sófalvi

Remembering
things you have said
and done.

Listening to classical music.

A bottle
of wine
chills in the fridge.
Waiting.
For us
to share.

Every day
brings
an awareness of
how little I know
of the overall scheme
of things.

How can you
appreciate pleasure
unless
you've experienced pain?

Life
unless you've been
faced with death?

What about
the light
at the end of the tunnel?

"If you can't
conquer the world...
settle for a little piece."

Dreams
often
brushed aside
could be realized.

Once in a while
a glimpse of
what could be.

Rózália Sófalvi

Ah...
wine.
Do your job.
Dull my senses.
Inspire me to write
but don't remind me
of my
loneliness.

Alibis & Lies

Once in the middle of the night
my phone rang.
"I need to see you.
I'll be there in seven minutes."

You entered my cluttered apartment.
Sat in the rocking chair.
Your long legs
stretched out before you.
You looked at me with those
wonderful, wicked eyes
I remember so fondly.
Like those of a child set free
in a candy store.
Or those of a tender
loving man.
I sat across the room from you
listening to your apologies
for the lateness
of your visit.

I did not protest.

Slowly
I rose from my chair.
Crossed the room to you.
Lowered myself
to the floor
at your feet.
Took your hands.
Laid them against my
glowing cheeks.
Turned my face and
kissed your palms.

You brushed a curl
from my eyes and
with your strong fingers
tangled in my hair
raised my face to you.

Your kiss, at first, was gentle
then more urgent,
bruising
as you gathered me
into your arms....

Everything
is not
the way
it seems.

Look at all the
lonely people in the world.

Pretending
they are not
lonely.

Time.
Endless.
Life
filled with unexpected
surprises.
Friendship.
Love.
Those do not vanish overnight.

Will we be lovers
will we be friends
when we are old?

Rózália Sófalvi

We would make a lovely
couple
holding
wrinkled hands.

Eyes sparkling
with hope and love....

Our children
would surely
know love.

Alibis & Lies

Examining dreams and reality.

I am a dreamer.
I fancy myself
living a life
of luxury and glamour
with the man I love.

I want to be someone special.
And it's frightening
to find
I am not.

I tell myself
we would be friends
under any
circumstances.

But you are gone.

Is that friendship?

Rózália Sófalvi

Confused.
I believed in you and me.

You make me angry.
I want to hit you.
I want to scream and cry.

You let me
fall in love with you
while you played
your little game.

You neglected to tell me
you were not a free man.

It was not a game.

How could it have felt so right?

Surely it's just the icy winter wind
that's wrapping you up so tight.

Surely
you'll be back
in the spring.

Rózália Sófalvi

Once upon a time
(in fairytales)
life used to be so simple.

But then
what would I dwell on
if you were here?

If everything was as I believed
it should be?

Eyes
staring off into space
once in awhile
catch someone
looking back.

Ah—
this is home.

Smoke stings my eyes.
The sound clutters my mind.
I could go—
but where?

This is home.

People
reaching out
but not touching.
Conversations collide or
go unheard.

Trying so hard not to mention your name.

Carol said what you did
... you did for yourself
alone.

Tried so hard
to avoid
that conclusion.
Tears fill my eyes.
Another illusion
shattered.

Reaching out
for a denial from you.

Surely I was right.
What you did
you did for me as well.

I remember touching you.

Alibis & Lies

Did I dream
the smoothness of your skin
your gentleness
the urgency of your hands
the touch of your lips
upon mine...

the feel of your hair against my face?

That's it!
It was
as it seemed to be.

Then.

- 155 -

Rózália Sófalvi

We all do the best we can
under the circumstances.

Don't give in
if you truly
believe
what you are doing
is right.

What I say
or do not say
does not matter
at all.

I once said
it was great
to feel.

Pain is a feeling.

Will I let it destroy me
or strengthen me?

It is impossible
to get
everything we want.

What would we do with it all?

But...

no one wants to be alone.

Rózália Sófalvi

Last night
we went to two movies—
my newest friend and I.
My reactions
would have been the same
with or without him.
It really did not matter.

I barely noticed him
sitting next to me
while Richard Chamberlain
was on the screen—
the tormented
classical pianist who
suffered and lived a lie
because
he loved men.

Alibis & Lies

Romance seems to have died.

I ask for nothing
yet my eyes
demand desperately
of those
who cannot give.

As the days go by
it gets
more and more difficult to be
without you.

My mind
craves
a debate.

My heart...
solitude.

Rózália Sófalvi

People pass by.
Their faces lost in a
blurry haze.

I miss you.

Nothing is clear while you are gone.

No one else matters.

No one else
brings
my mind to life.

Alibis & Lies

When innocence has died—
and there is
nowhere to hide...

who can I turn to?

When the magic is gone
and fear shatters
the peace and silence
my soul desires...

who can I turn to?

When love is gone
and with it
my sparkling eyes and smile...

who can I turn to?

Alone again.

But...

Rózália Sófalvi

I am
free to decide
where my life will lead.

Free
to select
the friends I want.
Discard
the ones
who do not inspire me.

Free
to choose lovers
who are gentle
or rough.
Retain the ones who please me most.

I am not fragile.
Be rough with me.

One solution
is to understand
my own desires.
Express my feelings
honestly.

I have survived this long
without you.
I'll damned well survive
without you from now on.

(If I must.)

I do not need
the aggravation.

Is it possible
I am wrong to be
so stubborn?

Alibis & Lies

They tell me
you have said goodbye.

No.

I will not shed a tear
for your departure.
Instead
I will smile.
And whisper a word
of thanks
for ever having known you.

Rózália Sófalvi

I have often thought…

if only
I had done
something differently
you would still be here.

If only
I had not gone
so eagerly
into your arms
you would still be here.

We would still be
good friends
that we were
instead of
the lovers we became.

We would still be
good friends
instead of
the strangers
we are now.

If only…
but then…

Alibis & Lies

I would not have felt
the stormy way
you touched me.
Watched your eyes approve.

I would not have heard
you whispering
my name
in the darkness.

I would not have watched
you
walking
away.

Rózália Sófalvi

All energy gone.
I fear
I loved
too hard.

Time.
Notches on the bedpost.
Conquests.
Defeat.
Anger.
Hatred.
Fear.
Disillusionment.
Tears.
Misplaced trust.

Alibis and lies.

Shining princes.
Princess.
Lost.

Rózália Sófalvi

Stand tall...
breathe deep
and put one foot
in front
of the other.

Tomorrow's
gonna be
a brand new
day.

The end again

... and

... a new beginning.